Prayers to
Close the Day

Pray much, and really from your heart:
Remember that prayer is the key
That opens the treasures of heaven.

St Mary Mazzarello

All readings based on Scripture and Saint Francis de Sales have been paraphrased, references are given as indications of source.

The clipart is from the internet site
Atlantic Fish http://www.geocities.com/chr4tp/index.htm

ISBN 0-9544539-8-0

© 2004 Don Bosco Publications
Charity Number 233779

Don Bosco Publications
Thornleigh House
Bolton BL1 6PQ
Tel 01204 308 811
Fax 01204 306868
www.don-bosco-publications.co.uk

DON BOSCO

Introduction

Salesian prayer is joyful, creative, simple and profound. It lends itself to community participation, is drawn from life experience and flows back into it.

This quotation from the Salesian Constitution 86 is an invitation to keep our prayer lively and available to sharing with others. For some time the need for an occasional alternative to *The Prayer of the Church* has been expressed from a number of individuals and groups. This book is an attempt to respond to that need, whilst still keeping a general shape that corresponds to *The Prayer of the Church*, but adds readings and some direct reflection on life experience that is central to Salesian spirituality. The format also offers the opportunity for faith-sharing where appropriate.

Prayers to Close the Day has been tested out in Salesian communities. It is offered to other individuals and groups for use in family, in communities and as a bedside prayer book for people of all ages. Using the reflections can help us to let go of the day, find meaning in what has happened and perhaps sleep more peacefully. The spirituality behind the prayers is based on the optimistic and gentle inspiration of St Francis de Sales. It challenges us to find God in the evening and grow in the awareness of God's abiding presence throughout the day.

Using the prayers

In prayer there is more listening to be done than speaking.

St Jane Frances de Chantal

The Leader
In group settings the leader's role is crucial in keeping a gentle pace to the prayer. In the text a 📖 symbol is used to indicate a pause. It is the leader's responsibility to set a rhythm to the prayer that suits the group and encourages reflection. The leader needs to choose the moment to conclude the reflection entitled, *Thinking about the Day* with a communal recitation of the offering prayer. The appropriate length of the silences needs to be sensed by the leader.

Choices
There are a number of choices available. Each person can choose one, or none, of the structured reflections for *Thinking about the Day*. The leader can choose to add one or two readings from the Salesian tradition at their own discretion. The intercessions can be used as in the text, or the members of the group can share their own prayers.

Faith-Sharing
A question has been added to the prayer format which could be the starting point for faith-sharing. In the normal pattern of community prayer there is usually not enough time for this. Where a longer evening prayer is needed, faith-sharing becomes possible. In the daily pattern of prayer the faith-sharing question is a further invitation to link life and prayer.

Saturday
The usual format is abandoned on Saturday, in favour of a simple reflection on the Gospel for Sunday, or other appropriate Gospel passages. This practice, sometime called *Lectio Divina* is encouraged by the Church as a preparation for the main liturgy of the week, on Sunday.

Week One

In quiet prayer, talk to God if you can.

If you can't, just stay there,

let God look at you,

and don't worry about anything.

St Francis de Sales

Week One

📖 indicates a pause for reflection

Leader's Greeting
As Sunday slips away
Our minds turn towards a new week
Where God waits to meet us. 📖

Come to us Lord this evening
Prepare us to recognise your presence
In the normal and novel events of a new week. 📖

Thinking about the Day   see pages 60 - 61.

Offering
Lord, I offer you a new and untouched week. Help me to unwrap this gift each day, with care and gratitude for all that it might bring. May I lose none of the hope it carries for new life and healing. Give me enough wisdom to uncover your Gospel plan in all that happens. 📖

Choral Prayer

1 Samuel 2

My life celebrates God's love
I find new heart in my God
No challenge or setback can change
The joy of knowing God's presence.

God alone knows the depths
Of each person's life story
It is useless to boast or pretend
Before God's rock-solid truth.

Those who trust in their own strength
Will find themselves weak and alone
Those who know their weakness
Will find a deeper strength in God.

It is God who lifts us from misery
And rescues us from the rubbish of each day
To place us among the fortunate
Who live hour by hour in God's presence.

Glory be to the Father...

Week One

Scripture Reading

Galatians 5:13

It is absolutely clear that we have been called by God to freedom. Please, don't make that freedom an excuse to do just what you want to do. Pleasing only yourself will destroy your freedom. Instead, use your freedom to serve others in love, because that is how the freedom of God's children will grow. The whole Gospel is summed up in the simple phrase; love others as you love yourself. ▭

Salesian Reading   Leader to choose from pages 62 - 68. ▭

Focus for Faith-Sharing

What are you looking forward to in the next week, and why? ▭

Magnificat   see page 59.

Intercessions

Lord, we pray for those who face this week with anxiety and fear.
R   May they find peace in your presence for what lies ahead.

Lord, we pray for those who start this week tired or hungry.
R   May they find strength in others, moved by your Gospel love.

Lord, we pray for young people, as a new week begins.
R   Increase their optimism and honesty, help them to grow in love.

Our Father

Final Prayer

Lord, stay with us as we begin a new, untouched week. As we unwrap the gift of each day, help us to trust you in all that we find, and give thanks for the privilege of living in your presence. We ask this through Christ, the Lord of all time, and our companion on each day's journey.

Amen

Blessing

Bless us with sleep that renews us in strength and faith.	**Amen**
Guide us in the week that lies before us.	**Amen**
Draw us close to yourself each day.	**Amen**

Week One

Monday

⌐ indicates a pause for reflection

Leader's Greeting

Thank you Lord for the touch of your hand
Calling me to peace and joy in your presence. ⌐

Thank you for staying with me
When I have lost balance and fallen flat on my face. ⌐

Thinking about the Day   see pages 60 - 61.

Offering

Lord, thank you for the gift of this day, for all the blessings it has brought. Forgive me when I have lost my balance today. When I have taken myself too seriously, lost my temper, or refused to learn or to relax with others. Help me to be more aware of your presence, and live with more balance tomorrow. ⌐

Choral Prayer

Philippians 4

I want you to be happy
Always happy in the Lord
I will say it again
I want you to be happy.

Let your openness be clear to everyone
Because your God is very close
There is no need for anxiety
Ask God for what you need.

Ask God with gratitude
And the peace of God
Will guard your hearts
And keep you close to Christ.

Fill all your waking hours
With what is good and honest
What is life-giving and worthy of praise
Then the God of peace will be with you.

Glory be to the Father…

Week One

Scripture Reading

Matthew 7:21

Jesus said 'It is not those who say to me *Lord! Lord!* that will live in the kingdom but those who do the will of my Father. Therefore, everyone who listens to my words and puts them into action is like the sensible builder who sets the house on rock. Rain may come, even floods and hurricanes and it will not fall because it is founded on rock.' 📖

Salesian Reading   Leader to choose from pages 62 - 68. 📖

Focus for Faith-Sharing
What keeps me balanced in life and spirit? 📖

Magnificat   see page 59.

Intercessions
For those who have lost their balance today through anger.
R Lord, bring them peace this evening.

For those who have become sad and depressed by the events of the day.
R Lord, renew their optimism and sense of purpose.

For those who have to carry anxieties and worries about health.
R Lord, reassure them of your presence in their struggle.

Our Father

Final Prayer
Lord, help us to live a balanced life tomorrow: close to you and yet in touch with others. Keep us active and involved with the serious business of building your kingdom, and yet cheerful too, because we are working to your wise plan. Help us to rest in peace tonight, and live gracefully in your presence tomorrow. **Amen**

Blessing
The Lord grant us a quiet night and a cheerful heart in the service of the Gospel. **Amen**

Week One

⌒ indicates a pause for reflection

Leader's Greeting
Thank you Lord for your presence
In the choices and the struggles of this day
For allowing me to stumble into you this evening. ⌒

Thank you for the gentleness
With which you surround me in this evening silence
May it penetrate and settle my thoughts and feelings. ⌒

Thinking about the Day   see pages 60 - 61.

Offering
Lord, I offer you this day, with all its challenges, opportunities and setbacks. May I accept both the success and failure I have met today. Help me to remember not to break the bruised reeds of the day, but deal gently with all that has happened. ⌒

Choral Prayer

Psalm 131

O Lord my heart is not proud
My eyes are not cold and hard.

I have not chased after things too great
Or let pride lead me to humiliation.

I have held myself, heart and soul
In silence and peace.

As a child clings in its mother's arms
So I cling in trust to a gentle God.

All people trust in the Lord
Cling to God now and forever.

Glory be to the Father...

Week One

Scripture Reading

Matthew 11:28
Tired? Worn out? Come to me you who are weary and exhausted with worries, and you will find peace and rest for your soul. Walk with me, work with me, learn from me. I am gentle and have a loving heart. Learn the unforced rhythms of grace. I will not lay upon you any burden too great for you. Come to me and learn to rest in my presence. ⌐

Salesian Reading   Leader to choose from pages 62 - 68. ⌐

Focus for Faith-Sharing
How has gentleness emerged in your thought and activity today? ⌐

Magnificat   see page 59.

Intercessions
Lord, we pray for those who are in need of the basic things in life.
R Help us to respond practically and raise awareness of their need.

Lord, we pray for all who have touched our lives in confusion or pain today.
R May we be honest and gentle with what is damaged in others.

Lord, we pray for those who must make a new start after a setback.
R May the courage of Mary at the cross inspire them for the future.

Our Father

Final Prayer
Lord, help us to trust your quiet and gentle presence. May we live in the rhythm of your goodness tomorrow, and find you in the quiet and simple pauses in our busy days. May we put others in touch with your presence through our gentleness and friendliness to all. **Amen**

Blessing
Be with us in the evening   *R With your gentleness*
As we see what we have achieved   *R Bring us your humility*
As we look towards a new day   *R Bring us your optimism*
And may Almighty God bless us, Father, Son and Spirit.   **Amen**

Week One

Wednesday

⌂ indicates a pause for reflection

Leader's Greeting
Thank you Lord for the gift of this day
For each moment that has made it unique
For each step shared in your presence. ⌂

Thank you for the times when you walked with me
Spoke to my heart and led me gently
Toward the most loving thing to do and be. ⌂

Thinking about the Day   see pages 60 - 61.

Offering
Father, thank you for the privilege of living with Jesus. Take this day and show me where my path has run alongside the way of Jesus. Help me to recognise where my heart has come to life in your love. Remind me this evening of your presence hidden in each day. ⌂

Choral Prayer
Psalm 23

God my shepherd
I do not need a thing
You have brought me to a place of rest.

True to your word
You have let me catch my breath
And shown me the right direction.

So even when the pathway
Dips into darkness I am not afraid
Because I know you are always at my side.

You refresh me and celebrate our friendship
In the sight of all my enemies and problems
You revive my spirits.

Your goodness and love
Pursue me through every day
And I will be at home in your presence forever.

Glory be to the Father...

Week One

Scripture Reading

John 10:11

I am the good shepherd, so I know my sheep and my sheep know me. In the same way I know the Father and the Father knows me. I put my sheep before me, sacrificing myself if necessary. The true shepherd walks right up to the sheep and they are not afraid. They follow him because they recognise his voice. They don't follow a stranger's voice, but will scatter, because they don't know his voice. ⌐⌐

Salesian Reading   Leader to choose from pages 62 - 68. ⌐⌐

Focus for Faith-Sharing

In what way have I lived with Jesus today? ⌐⌐

Magnificat   see page 59.

Intercessions

Lord, thank you for your living presence and walking with us every day.
R Help us to learn the lessons that this day has brought.

Lord, I offer you each person that has shared my journey through this day.
R Help me to recognise your presence in them.

Lord, I thank you for those people who have been difficult with me today.
R May I see, in them, a chance to live your patient love for us all.

Our Father

Final Prayer

Father in heaven, we thank you for the presence of your Son Jesus, who has walked with us throughout this day. Help us to live with Jesus every moment cheerfully confident that in Him, all will be well. May we leave our troubles safely in your hands tonight, and rest in the presence of Jesus who lives and reigns for ever and ever. **Amen**

Blessing

May you find peace in your heart   *R The peace of Christ*
May you find rest for your soul   *R In the presence of Christ*
May you leave all worry behind   *R In the providence of Christ*

Week One

Thursday

📖 indicates a pause for reflection

Leader's Greeting
Thank you Lord for a day
Filled with opportunities
To put love into action. 📖

Thank you for your abiding presence
Living in other people
And your love alive in me today. 📖

Thinking about the Day   see pages 60 - 61.

Offering
Lord, thank you for another day of life. Thank you for the chance to immerse myself in your loving kindness, in prayer, activity and in relationship with others. Take everything I have done and give it a place in your plan of love. 📖

Choral Prayer
Corinthians 13

Aim for the gifts that really matter
Keep looking for the best gift of all
The gift of love.

If I am clever with words
But speak without love
It is all empty noise.

If I can predict what will happen
And penetrate deep mysteries
Without love I am still nothing.

Love is always patient and kind
Avoids jealousy and boasting
And is never rude or selfish.

Real love does not enjoy others' failures
But chooses to excuse them
And to hope and trust in the future.

Glory be to the Father…

Week One

Scripture Reading

Luke 6:27

Love the ones whom you call enemies. Show kindness to those who target you with hatred. Pray for those who treat you badly. If someone slaps you on one side of the face offer them the other side too. If someone takes your coat, offer him your jacket too. Give to everyone who asks, and treat others as you would wish to be treated yourself. If you only love those who love you, what thanks do you deserve?

Salesian Reading Leader to choose from pages 62 - 68. 📖

Focus for Faith-Sharing

How has my heart been moved to love and compassion today? 📖

Magnificat see page 59.

Intercessions

R Lord, show them your love today.

For those who do not know that they are loved. **R**

For those who cannot show love to others. **R**

For those in our community who do not feel loved this evening. **R**

For young people and parents, starved of love in their homes. **R**

Our Father

Final Prayer

Father in heaven, help us to recognise your love in unlikely places. Teach us to be sensitive to your promptings, in relationship to others. Keep us generous and balanced in our affections. Make us grow in the wisdom that comes from knowing that we are loved unconditionally and forever. We ask this through Christ Our Lord. **Amen**

Blessing

May the Lord live in our hearts, in the love we show to others. **Amen**
May God give us love and kindness, to share tomorrow. **Amen**
May God bless each of us with restful hearts tonight. **Amen**

Week One

Friday

📖 indicates a pause for reflection

Leader's Greeting
R *Thank you, Lord.*
For the breath of your Spirit, moving through us today. **R**
For your presence, in difficulty and challenge. **R**
For your peaceful hidden presence, in heart and mind. **R**
For Mary, who believed and conceived in your presence. **R**
For this moment of peace. **R**

Thinking about the Day see pages 60 - 61.

Offering
Lord, I offer you the day that is almost over. Into your hands I commend all the words and actions that have made the pattern of this day unique. May I, like Mary, ponder on all that has happened, and treasure the experience of living another day in your presence. 📖

Choral Prayer
Luke 1

Praise God in the story of all people
A God who has made his home among us
A saviour who would free us from all that holds us back
From deeper friendship with God.

His presence brings a time of justice
A time of holiness and freedom from fear
Just as Abraham had been promised.

A child will become a prophet
And open up a new way
Into friendship with God.

A relationship of forgiveness
That draws us into the loving kindness
At the heart of God's life.

A life that casts the darkness from our lives
And guides us into the path of peace.

Glory be to the Father...

Week One

Scripture Reading

Luke 2:46
Having found Jesus in the temple Mary said to him, *Young man, why have you done this to us? We have been so worried looking for you.* Jesus replied, *Why were you looking for me? You must have realised that I would be here, dealing with the work of my Father.* Mary and Joseph did not understand what he was talking about. Jesus went back home with them obediently. Mary stored these things in her heart and thought about them often, as treasured insights into her Son's life. 📖

Salesian Reading
Leader to choose from pages 62 - 68. 📖

Focus for Faith-Sharing
In what ways have you walked in God's presence today? 📖

Magnificat
see page 59.

Intercessions
For those who, in sadness, feel deserted by God.
R May they find hope through Mary at the foot of the cross.

For those who cannot cope with change.
R May they find strength in the confusion of Mary at the Annunciation.

For those who have come close to death.
R May Mary, who saw her husband and Son die, give them the hope of Resurrection.

Our Father

Final Prayer
Lord, help us to find in Mary the inspiration to live the ordinary patterns of life deeply and reflectively. May Mary's instinct, to welcome your presence, become part of our own way of living. May your presence be woven through all our work, and help to build a community that makes your kingdom visible. We ask this through Christ our Lord.

Amen

Blessing
Mary, help of all people.   *R Pray for us*

Week One

Saturday

This is a slow contemplative praying of the Sunday scripture that leads towards union with God, and is an ideal way of preparing for tomorrow's Eucharist. Its simplicity helps to uncover some of the spiritual rhythms at work in our lives. The prayer rests on an ability to listen to scripture with the heart and *hear the still small voice of God.* (1 Kings 19:12)

Opening Prayer
Lord, open my ears to hear your word. May these moments of silence help me to recognise your presence calling me to life. Calm my heart and mind with your still small voice. **Amen**

How the word touches me
The Gospel passage for Sunday is read aloud twice with a brief pause between readings. Listeners notice some segment or word from the passage that attracts them. A brief silence follows. The group is invited to share, without explanation, the word or phrase that attracted them.

How the word speaks to me
The passage is read aloud again by a different person. Silence follows for reflection on, *Where do these words touch my life today?* All are invited to share briefly on what connections the story makes with their lives.

How am I challenged?
The passage is read again by a third voice. Silence follows, reflecting on the phrase, *these words challenge me to......in the days that lie ahead.* A longer sharing follows.

Ending
The leader invites the group to pray in silence for those on either side of them.

Final Prayer
Thank you Lord, for your abiding presence in each person's life, and in these words of scripture. Stay with us this evening and help us to rest in your presence tonight. **Amen**

Other Scripture texts to use: St Matthew's Gospel

Weeds	13:24-30
Paralysed Child	9:1-8
Beatitudes	5:1-12
Sowing Seed	13:4-9
Walking on Water	14:22-33
A rich youth	19:16-22

Week Two

*Nothing done in a huge rush or impulsively
is ever really done well.*

St Francis de Sales

Week Two

Sunday

indicates a pause for reflection

Leader's Greeting
As the sun sets on the weekend
We come in peace
To the Lord of all life.

Be with us on the border
Between work and rest
Help us to move gracefully into a new week.

Thinking about the Day   see pages 60 - 61.

Offering
Lord, I offer you a brand new week. Help me to live gracefully through all that will happen. Make my mind and heart ready to receive the blessing you will scatter through each day. Give me a heart, generous enough to be a blessing for others in the week that is waiting.

Choral Prayer
Psalm 118

I thank God for a goodness that never ends
I thank God for a love that lasts.

When I am under pressure God is always close
And I find no need for fear
Who can do me lasting harm
When God is my helper?

It is better to take refuge in God
Than to trust in power or popularity
But even when I lose my balance
God will never let me go.

Thank you Lord for your wisdom
Holding everything together
What everyone else rejected as rubbish
You have turned into a keystone.

Glory be to the Father...

Week Two

Scripture Reading

Luke 20:27

I will give you an inner guide, the Spirit, who will remind you of my word written in your heart. Peace is my gift to you, my own inner peace is my parting gift. It is not a peace that the world can give, it is my personal gift to each of you. So do not let your hearts be troubled or afraid. I am going away but I shall return. I have said this before it happens, to help you to believe and trust the Father in all that takes place. 📖

Salesian Reading   Leader to choose from pages 62 - 68. 📖

Focus for Faith-Sharing

What will be your key to living close to God in the week ahead? 📖

Magnificat   see page 59.

Intercessions

Lord, make us aware of the key moments that will mark our journey with you in the week ahead.
R   Keep us sensitive to your presence calling us into life.

Keep us, Lord, close to those who will struggle with this week's events through sadness and disappointment.
R   May our support strengthen their faith in you.

We pray that we will have the courage to live the Gospel this week.
R   When challenged may we be honest in living your love and justice.

Our Father

Final Prayer

Lord, stay with us on the border of a new week. With all its uncertainty and challenge it is the place where we are called to meet you on our journey. Keep us sensitive to your presence, especially in what is rejected in the week ahead. Make us ready to challenge whatever works against the peace and compassion of your kingdom.

Amen

Blessing

Breathe your peace into the week ahead.   **Amen**
Give us courage to live in your kingdom.   **Amen**

Week Two

Monday

⌘ indicates a pause for reflection

Leader's Greeting
Thank you Lord for your presence
For the scattered touches of your life
In ordinary humdrum routines. ⌘

Thank you for the predictable things
That give me space to remember you
Thank you for this peaceful evening moment. ⌘

Thinking about the Day   see pages 60 - 61.

Offering
Lord, I offer you this day. Thank you for your presence in the routine
rhythms of the day. Keep me focussed on the mystery at the heart of
daily living. Help me uncover your face in both friends and enemies, and
keep me in touch with your life in stillness and storm. ⌘

Choral Prayer
Psalm 127

If the Lord does not work with us
Our work will never last
If God does not protect our efforts
Then our energy is wasted.

It is useless to get up early
And to work your fingers to the bone
Don't you know that your real success
Is simply a gift from God?

Don't you see that it's people that count?
God's best gift to us is one another
Like a quiver full of arrows
God's children can meet any challenge.

You are blessed through your parents
And through your children
Nothing can shake the confidence of those
Who build on the presence of the Lord.

Glory be to the Father...

Week Two

Scripture Reading

Matthew 5:27

If God pays so much attention to the wild flowers, that are here today and thrown away tomorrow, don't you think God will also pay attention to you, and do the best for you? Don't you see that you can be so busy about earning and owning things, that you miss what God wants to give to you free of charge? People who don't know God get worried about everything. But you know God, and how God works in little things. So don't worry about what you need. Your Father knows what you need and you will not be forgotten. ⌂

Salesian Reading   Leader to choose from pages 62 - 68. ⌂

Focus for Faith-Sharing
How does God touch my heart most often in my daily life? ⌂

Magnificat   see page 59.

Intercessions
Lord, we believe you have entered our world and history.
R Help us to find you in the story of this day.

Lord, we pray for those who have lost a sense of the sacred in their lives.
R May you surprise them with a sense of your presence today.

Lord, we pray for those whose ordinary life is difficult and dark.
R May your presence unfold hope and new life in their hearts.

Our Father

Final Prayer
Lord, help us to see you in the ordinary, and the routine events of all our days. Transform the timetable of our day with the seeds of Resurrection, planted in quiet moments, so that the work we have done today may lead to an eternal richness. We ask this through Christ our Lord. **Amen**

Blessing
Lord of the small and ordinary moments, bless us with simplicity of heart and peace this night and always. **Amen**

Week Two

Tuesday

☐ indicates a pause for reflection

Leader's Greeting
Thank you Lord, for walking with me today
From the earliest hour until this moment of peace. ☐

Thank you for the signs of your presence
Marking my journey today
And the gentle nudging of your Spirit
In my wayward heart. ☐

Thinking about the Day   see pages 60 - 61.

Offering
In this evening hour Lord, I bring to you my body, my heart and my mind.
Talk to me about the day that is ending, and help me learn how to walk
each day a little closer to you. I offer back to you all those moments
where you have nudged my Spirit, and invited me into partnership with
you. ☐

Choral Prayer
Psalm 127
Lord, you know my heart, your evidence is first hand
I am an open book to you
You know my every thought from miles away
Before I say a word you know what will be said.

I look over my shoulder and there you are
Your reassuring presence surrounds me
I cannot take it in.

Could I ever avoid your presence?
Is there any place that is out of your sight?
Whether I am underground or in the stars
Or if I flew to a far horizon and into darkness
You would find me in a minute.

You made me body and soul and you know me
You know how I was shaped from childhood
My life is laid out like a map in your presence
You know me better than I know myself.

Glory be to the Father…

Week Two

Scripture Reading

Matthew 25:35

I was starving and you gave me a meal
I was thirsty and you gave me a drink
I was homeless and you took me in
I was shivering and you gave me warm clothes
I was sick in prison and you came to me
Whenever you did these things to the least of my brothers and sisters
You did it to me. 📖

Salesian Reading   Leader to choose from pages 62 - 68. 📖

Focus for Faith-Sharing
When did I feel closest to God today? 📖

Magnificat   see page 59.

Intercessions
Lord, we pray for our community and friends.
R   That we may recognise in ordinary lives the eternal life you offer.

Lord, we pray for those who have suffered insults and prejudice today.
R   May they recognise their God-given dignity whatever happens.

Lord, we pray for those who have drawn strength from us today.
R   May our prayer bring them peace this evening.

Our Father

Final Prayer
Lord, stay with us this evening and be with us as we plan for a new day.
May our struggles and our successes never separate us from your
abiding presence. **Amen**

Blessing
May the Lord bless us with quiet hearts and minds this evening. **Amen**

Week Two

⌑ indicates a pause for reflection

Leader's Greeting
Thank you for the gifts of this day
Filled with a thousand trivial trials
And little opportunities. ⌑

Thank you for the strength I borrow from you Lord
In those scattered moments
When I recognised your presence
And responded as best as I could. ⌑

Thinking about the Day   see pages 60 - 61.

Offering
I offer you the silence of these evening moments. Accept all I am at the end of this day. Take the little deaths that I must die, from moment to moment, and weave them into your eternal Resurrection. ⌑

Choral Prayer
Psalm 116

I love God
Because he hears me when I call
He bends down to listen to my cares.

Things were closing in on me
Distress gripped my heart
And I called on God's name.

Return to your rest my soul
For God will treat you kindly.

He has rescued me from death
And kept my feet from stumbling.

So I will trust even when I realise
I am crushed by disappointment.

Glory be to the Father…

Week Two

Scripture Reading

Matthew 6:25

That is why I am telling you not to worry about your life, what you are to eat, nor about your body and what you are to wear. Surely life means more than food, and the body more than clothing? Your heavenly Father knows you need both. So set your hearts on God's kingdom first, and on right living, and these other things will be given to you. So do not worry about tomorrow; tomorrow will take care of itself. 📖

Salesian Reading   Leader to choose from pages 62 - 68. 📖

Focus for Faith-Sharing

What anxieties lead you to lose a sense of God's presence? 📖

Magnificat   see page 59.

Intercessions

R Trust, surrender, believe, receive.

Lord, help us to end this day in peace.   **R**

Lord, help us to let go of any disappointments at the end of this day. **R**

Help us to leave the outcome of our work today to your providence. **R**

Help us to stay optimistic and cheerful in the service of the young. **R**

As we sleep tonight, teach us the wisdom this day has brought.   **R**

Our Father

Final Prayer

Lord, stay with us this evening, help us to put this day back in your hands. May your peace settle our hearts and your wisdom grow within us. Help us to use the experience of today into a wiser tomorrow, and a richer following of your Gospel. We ask this through Jesus our risen Lord. **Amen**

Blessing

May God bless us with peaceful hearts.   **Amen**
May he increase our trust in his providence.   **Amen**
May God leave us quiet and at home in his presence tonight. **Amen**

Week Two

Thursday

📖 indicates a pause for reflection

Leader's Greeting

Leader: We gather in the peace of God's presence.
R *To collect the fragments of this day.*
Leader: We rest in the silence of God's presence.
R *To hear the mystery we have lived today.*
Leader: We gather in the wisdom of God's presence.
R *To learn the lessons of this day.* 📖

Thinking about the Day   see pages 60 - 61.

Offering

Lord, I offer you this day and all the energy and optimism that it has carried. I offer you all my hopes and dreams. Renew and focus my life according to your dream for me. Keep me in touch with the energy and optimism of youth, even as I grow older in wisdom and experience. 📖

Choral Prayer

Psalm 8

Amazing Lord and God
Your name is everywhere
Written through all creation
Little children sing about you.

Toddlers delight in your creation
Silencing the cynicism of godless hearts
I look up at the sky and am lost in space
Then I see myself in perspective
And wonder why you care about me at all.

Yet we are little less than gods in your eyes
You have put us in charge of this world
Made us stewards of all creation.

The cattle, the birds, the fish of the sea
Are all placed in our care by you
Our amazing Lord and God.

Glory be to the Father...

Week Two

Scripture Reading
1 Timothy 4:12
It is urgent that the good news is heard. Don't let anyone put you down just because you are young. Witness to the Gospel with your life: by word and action, by love, by faith and by integrity. Stay close to scripture, give good advice and keep that special gift for ministry fresh and active each day. ▱

Salesian Reading
Leader to choose from pages 62 - 68. ▱

Focus for Faith-Sharing
In what ways did you experience God as youthful today? ▱

Magnificat
see page 59.

Intercessions
R Keep them in your loving kindness
For young people who struggle in school.   *R*

For young people who hope to change the world.   *R*

For young people exploring relationships.   *R*

For young people searching for meaning in life.   *R*

When family life is hard for young people.   *R*

When friends let young people down.   *R*

When the temptation to excess is strong.   *R*

When joy and peace seem far away.   *R*

Our Father

Final Prayer
Lord, young people are both precious and vulnerable as they grow towards maturity, help us to offer them support, guidance and good example. Let us see the grace of your presence in their lives, and show us how to encourage their goodness. We ask this through Christ Our Lord. **Amen**

Blessing
May the Lord keep us safe and give us rest, and bring us to peace at the end of this day. **Amen**

Week Two

Friday

⌂ indicates a pause for reflection

Leader's Greeting
Lord, let us know the shortness of life
That we might gain wisdom of heart
And find peace in your eternal plans for us. ⌂

Be with us as we end this day
Give us peace and truth as we think over what has happened
Give us compassion that we may grow in wisdom of heart. ⌂

Thinking about the Day   see pages 60 - 61.

Offering
Lord, I offer you this day and all that has been achieved through both success and failure. Thank you for the lessons of love hidden in the ordinary events of this day and for being a teacher who stays close to us as we learn. ⌂

Choral Prayer
Psalm 49

Listen everyone rich and poor alike
If you have your feet on the ground listen
I offer you wisdom, plain and simple
From the experience of your life.

I have tuned my ear to wisdom
And played out my problems on the harp
So why should I fear difficult times
When life knocks me off balance.

There is no easy escape from setbacks
No one is immune to shock and failure
Everyone knows that the best of us die
And the grave becomes our home.

So don't be impressed by success
It can't take you beyond the grave
It is God that rescues us from death
And give us life that lasts.

Glory be to the Father...

Week Two

Scripture Reading

Isaiah 44:1

I have been here for people who were not even looking for me, it is the Lord that speaks. I kept saying, *I am here, in front of you.* But they did not see or hear me. I reached out, day after day, and yet people turned their backs. Instead they followed their own whims and wanted to do things their own way, as if I had nothing to offer them. But I will support those who recognise me and not destroy the whole people. All the people will be blessed in those who hear my voice. 📖

Salesian Reading   Leader to choose from pages 62 - 68. 📖

Focus for Faith-Sharing

What lessons has God taught me today? 📖

Magnificat   see page 59.

Intercessions

We pray for wisdom for parents as they bring up their children.
R May they recognise God's presence in their sons and daughters.

We pray for wisdom for teachers and all educators.
R May their work uncover God's life at the heart of each student.

We pray for those who face failure and illness.
R May they see, in setbacks, the opportunity to grow in wisdom.

Our Father

Final Prayer

Lord, stay with us as we draw to the end of another day. Let your Gospel wisdom open up the meaning of this day. Help us to leave all our uncertainties in the safety of your certain love, and rest in your wisdom with grateful hearts tonight. We ask this through Christ Our Lord. **Amen**

Blessing

Lord, make us wise through trusting you. **Amen**
Keep us trusting by knowing you. **Amen**
Help us to know you by loving your wisdom. **Amen**

Week Two

Saturday

This is a slow contemplative praying of the Sunday scripture that leads towards union with God, and is an ideal way of preparing for tomorrow's Eucharist. Its simplicity helps to uncover some of the spiritual rhythms at work in our lives. The prayer rests on an ability to listen to scripture with the heart and *hear the still small voice of God.* (1 Kings 19:12)

Opening Prayer
Lord, open my ears to hear your word. May these moments of silence help me to recognise your presence calling me to life. Calm my heart and mind with your still small voice. **Amen**

How the word touches me
The Gospel passage for Sunday is read aloud twice with a brief pause between readings. Listeners notice some segment or word from the passage that attracts them. A brief silence follows. The group is invited to share, without explanation, the word or phrase that attracted them.

How the word speaks to me
The passage is read aloud again by a different person. Silence follows for reflection, *Where do these words touch my life today?* All are invited to share briefly on what connections the story makes with their lives.

How am I challenged?
The passage is read again by a third voice. Silence follows, reflecting on the phrase, *these words challenge me to......in the days that lie ahead.* A longer sharing follows.

Ending
The leader invites the group to pray in silence for those on either side of them.

Final Prayer
Thank you Lord, for your abiding presence in each person's life, and in these words of scripture. Stay with us this evening and help us to rest in your presence tonight. **Amen**

Other Scripture texts to use: St Mark's Gospel

Bartimaeus	10:46-52
Calming a storm	4:35-41
Children	10:13-16
Transfigured	9:2-8
Going Home	6:1-6
Parables	4:21-32

Week Three

*Remember God's presence as often as
you can and notice what God is doing
and what you are doing.*

St Francis de Sales

Week Three

Sunday

⌂ indicates a pause for reflection

Leader's Greeting
Lord of the evening
Prepare us for a new week
Of working with you. ⌂

Ease our anxieties, build up our energy
Let your face shine upon us
In the events of another week. ⌂

Thinking about the Day   see pages 60 - 61.

Offering
Lord of all history, I offer you a new week with all its routine and uncertainty. Make it an adventure into a stronger partnership with you. May this prayer help me recognise the face of God more clearly in those I will meet. Lord, let the light of your face shine through this week. ⌂

Choral Prayer
Psalm 4

God, who protects and guards me
Guide me when I am confused
When I am troubled hear my struggles
And listen to my prayer.

There are so many ways to be deluded
So many lies that look like truth
My heart is easily confused
And my mind closed off from your wisdom.

Lord, you never let me down
Though I do not understand your ways
In the evening help me reflect in peace
And bow before your wisdom.

Lord, let the light of your face
Shine on my life with peace
And I will sleep soundly
In your saving presence.

Glory be to the Father...

Week Three

Scripture Reading

John 14:16

I will give you a guide for the journey, to be with you forever. It is a Spirit that others will not be able to see or understand. But you will understand and recognise this Spirit of truth because it is with you and inside you every day. I have not left you orphans. Anyone who loves me will be loved by my Father and I shall show myself to them. ⌐

Salesian Reading Leader to choose from pages 62 - 68. ⌐

Focus for Faith-Sharing
How has the light of God's face shone on my life today? ⌐

Magnificat see page 59.

Intercessions
Lord, be a light for us on the journey through a new week.
R Keep us faithful to your guidance in the coming week.

Lord, help us to be a light to others in the week ahead.
R May we radiate your honest love to all we meet.

Lord, we pray for all those who begin this week with darkened hearts.
R May they find hope and strength to lighten their burdens.

Our Father

Final Prayer
Lord, let the light of your face shine upon all that we do in the week ahead. Keep us free from shame to live in your presence. May our lives reflect the light of your face into the darkness and confusion of this world. We ask this through Christ, the light of the world. **Amen**

Blessing
Lord, dispel the darkness of this night.   **Amen**
Drive far away the shadows of insecurity.   **Amen**
Let the light of your face shine on us in the coming week. **Amen**

Week Three

Monday

ᴇᴀ indicates a pause for reflection

Leader's Greeting
Lord, bring us peace and calm at the end of this day
Slow the breath of busyness
Be with us in the silence. ᴇᴀ

Open up the mystery of this day
For our highest destiny
Lies in our daily living. ᴇᴀ

Thinking about the Day   see pages 60 - 61.

Offering
Lord, I offer you this day. Thank you for the shared journey of this day.
With all its routine and disappointment it is the holy ground on which I
walk with you, my God. Gather up what is of value and help me to let go
of what is not worthy of a child of God. ᴇᴀ

Choral Prayer
Psalm 46

Response:
The God of all history is with us. The Lord of our story gives us
strength.

God is a safe place to live
A constant support in times of trouble
When we stand on the brink of disaster
We can still look ahead with confidence. **R**

Rivers and fountains of God's presence
Flow through my daily life
I look for the signs of God's presence
In the growth of plants and people. **R**

Watch for the signs of peace
Breaking out in ordinary lives
Stand back and look for God
Within and beyond all you see. **R**

Glory be to the Father…

Week Three

Scripture Reading

Romans 8:14
Those who are moved by The Spirit are the sons and daughters of God. The Spirit does not tie us down, but sets us free to cry out *Abba, Father!* The same Spirit joins with our spirit to confirm that we really are the children of God. If we are God's children, then we are also in line to share with Christ the inheritance that is available only through his death and resurrection.

Salesian Reading   Leader to choose from pages 62 - 68. ⌐

Focus for Faith-Sharing
Have I lived the day with confidence in a loving Father? ⌐

Magnificat   see page 59.

Intercessions
Lord, we pray for our community at the end of this day.
R May we remember that we are brothers and sisters with a Father in heaven.

Lord, help those for whom the day has been filled with disappointment.
R May they remain in touch with God as Father, and grow in confidence as children of God.

Lord, we pray for young people who have lost confidence in their parents.
R May they recognise the goodness of God in their family.

Our Father

Final Prayer
Stay with us Lord this evening. As we look back at the day we have lived in your presence, give us the grace to see your family likeness unfolding in others. May the faces of all those we live and work with, bring us closer to you. We ask this through Christ Our Lord. **Amen**

Blessing
Lord, let the light of your face shine upon us.
R And we shall rest in your peace at the end of this day.

Week Three

Tuesday

⌂ indicates a pause for reflection

Leader's Greeting
Jesus breathes peace on his friends at the end of the day
May the peace of God settle in our hearts
And bring us to rest in the Spirit. ⌂

Spirit of God breathe through the challenges of this day
Let your peace bring order to our hearts and minds
Remind us that we are always safe in your presence. ⌂

Thinking about the Day   see pages 60 - 61.

Offering
Lord, you have walked with me today, as a friend and guide. I offer you
the successes and failures of this day. Help me to follow your guidance
tomorrow. Show me how to follow the map of the Gospel, and feel the
tug of your Spirit drawing me in the right direction. ⌂

Choral Prayer
Psalm 43

Stand by me Lord
Be my protector, my guide
Shield me from the cynical
From the delusions that surround me.

Lord I am so alone and lost
Without your presence to guide me
Give me a map and a compass
To find my way back to your presence.

Then I can face any challenge
And draw strength from my God.

Why am I so helpless
So low in spirits?
Let me trust the Lord again
And praise God's wisdom in all things.

Glory be to the Father...

Week Three

Scripture Reading

1 Peter 1:13

Keep yourself ready for action in the service of God. Stay alert and sensitive in every situation. Hold your focus on the hope you feel in the promises and blessings of Jesus Christ. Be faithful to the way God is moving in your life. Don't let the pressures and problems of the day push your life out of shape. Avoid falling back into the pattern you lived before you came to know the reality of God.

Salesian Reading
Leader to choose from pages 62 - 68. ⌓

Focus for Faith-Sharing
How has God been my map and compass today? ⌓

Magnificat
see page 59.

Intercessions
Lord, we pray for those who have lost their way in the confusion of a difficult day.
R   May they find your peace and wisdom this evening.

Lord, we pray for married couples young and old.
R   May their journey be a sign of the partnership God offers to us each day.

Lord, we pray tonight for young people, lost in a maze of life choices.
R   Help them hear your Spirit calling them, to know and use their gifts to build a better world.

Our Father

Final Prayer
Lord, be a constant guide on our journey. We need your patience as we struggle to know and do your will. Help us to trust, even when fear and frustration throw us into confusion. Stay close to each of us now, as Father, Son and Spirit and help us rest in your love this night and always.
Amen

Blessing
May the Father confirm us as children of God.   **Amen**
May the Son inspire us to follow the Gospel.   **Amen**
May the Spirit renew us tonight in the service of God.   **Amen**

Week Three

Wednesday

indicates a pause for reflection

Leader's Greeting
Bring us to peace in this evening hour Lord
And place us on the solid ground of your presence
After the activity of the day.

Teach us to sit in patience
In the silence of your love
So that your plans and timetables
May emerge again in our lives.

Thinking about the Day   see pages 60 - 61.

Offering
The day you gave is almost over, and I return it to you with gratitude, for all you have achieved through my success and failure. Help me to see the promises of resurrection, beneath the surface of even the most lifeless moments of the day. May I live by faith, that your Resurrection will eventually reach every corner of my life.

Choral Prayer

Psalm 40

I waited and waited for the Lord
And finally God noticed me and listened
He pulled me out of my misery
And out of the dark circle of my thoughts.

He put me down on solid ground
And gave me back the confidence I had lost
God drew me deeper into love
And taught me how to celebrate life again.

The people that turn to God find real happiness
And see through life to a deeper meaning
The whole of creation is brimming with God
For those who have courage to look.

God is gloriously hidden in and beyond creation
But our words dry up before God's mystery.

Glory be to the Father…

Week Three

Scripture Reading

Romans 10:8
The message of God must live in your heart and be active in what you do and say. Your life will take on its proper shape, only if you witness to God in the way you live and speak. Life will only have lasting meaning if you believe in your heart that Jesus was raised from the dead. Your heart has only to believe, and your life to witness to the resurrection, for you to share eternal life. ⌒

Salesian Reading   Leader to choose from pages 62 - 68. ⌒

Focus for Faith-Sharing
Where has the solid ground of God's love been for you today? ⌒

Magnificat   see page 59.

Intercessions
We pray for those who carry the burden of grief tonight.
R May they find hope and comfort in the Resurrection story.

We pray for those who feel betrayed by friends.
R May they find in God the faithfulness they need, to rebuild their trust in life.

We pray for young people who have no confidence in their gifts.
R Lord, send them people who can affirm their goodness.

We pray for our divided and unjust world.
R May our lives be moved, beyond comfort, to build God's kingdom of peace.

Our Father

Final Prayer
Lord, may your Resurrection find a welcome in our hearts and radiate hope to others in our actions. Make us signs and bearers of your love to those around us. Tomorrow, help us to be ready to live out the optimism of the Gospel message. We ask this in the name of Jesus our risen Lord. **Amen**

Blessing
May the Lord bless you with peace at the end of the day. **Amen**
May the Resurrection be a reality in your life. **Amen**
May your confidence grow in the service of the Gospel. **Amen**

Week Three

Thursday

⌒ indicates a pause for reflection

Leader's Greeting
Lord, we bring you the bits and pieces of our day
The broken plans and promises
The best and the worst of all that has happened. ⌒

We open our hands to you and offer the day to you
Take what needs to be changed, discard what is of no value
Help us to recognise what is of lasting value. ⌒

Thinking about the Day   see pages 60 - 61.

Offering
Lord, I offer you the best and the worst of this day. Take it and make it
part of your Cross and Resurrection story, and part of the Gospel pattern
in my life. Help me to trust you tonight with the things that don't make
sense and keep me patient with myself. ⌒

Choral Prayer

Psalm 32

You are blessed to have a fresh start
To have God wipe out past mistakes
When guilt is kept locked inside
Both body and spirit pay the price.

When I did not hide from my guilt
When I faced my failures honestly
Then my Lord forgave and forgot
And welcomed me back home.

So let us be honest with our God
About our mistakes and motivations
Whatever troubles come to our door
God can be trusted to cope with them all.

Don't be like a stubborn mule
Refusing the guidance of God
Trust in God in times of trouble
Make the Lord your hiding place.

Glory be to the Father…

Week Three

Scripture Reading

Colossians 3:12

You are members of God's own family. You are loved and chosen to be close to God in all that happens. So live out that family likeness by being patient, understanding, full of loving kindness and compassion. Look out for the needs of others and offer practical help. When arguments break out, be ready to forgive one another, as soon as you can. Live the forgiveness and compassion that we have seen in the life of Jesus Christ Our Lord.

Salesian Reading   Leader to choose from pages 62 - 68. 📖

Focus for Faith-Sharing
How do I hide from my guilt? 📖

Magnificat   see page 59.

Intercessions
R Give us new hope in our daily living.

When we feel we have got nowhere at the end of the day. *R*
When we fail to live up to our own expectations.   *R*
When people disappoint us and let us down.   *R*
When we fail to see hope in what we are doing.   *R*
When family and friends seem absent.   *R*
When we feel helpless about injustice.   *R*
When health and energy fail.   *R*

Our Father

Final Prayer
Lord of the universe and Lord of each life, be with us this evening. Keep us searching for the patterns and themes of Resurrection, in the story of this day. May we be faithful to the Easter mystery at work in our lives, and allow it to shape our minds and hearts. Help us to spread the influence of your kingdom to a needy world. We ask this through the risen Jesus, Our Lord. **Amen**

Blessing
May the Lord bless our lives.   *R With the gift of his presence.*
May God open our hearts.   *R To recognise Resurrection now.*
May Easter never be far away.   *R And sustain us in hard times.*

Week Three

Friday

⌓ indicates a pause for reflection

Leader's Greeting
Lord, we gather with silent hands the threads of the day
We offer you the loose ends of all that has happened. ⌓

Help us to recognise your hand
Weaving its pattern of love through this closing day. ⌓

Thinking about the Day   see pages 60 - 61.

Offering
Lord, I offer you this day and the strands of your Spirit that have run through each moment. Thank you for your intimacy in my life, and the daily opportunity for partnership with you. Take the unfinished work of my day and use it to build your kingdom. ⌓

Choral Prayer
Psalm 31

Lord, I need a place to hide tonight
Please don't let me down.

In your goodness listen to me
Make sense of what is happening.

I am surrounded by confusion Lord
Tempted to make the wrong choices.

You know my inside story Lord
The troubles and sadness I live with.

I put my life into your hands
I put my trust in you alone.

Love the Lord all you people
Trust our God who never gives up on us.

Glory be to the Father...

Week Three

Scripture Reading

Ephesians 2:5

With an immense compassion and an incredible love, God took our lives, deadened by sin, and embraced us with kindness. It was done with no help from us, it was a total gift, nothing for us to feel clever about at all. God picked us up, and put us alongside the risen Jesus. Our lives now make sense because of God's goodness. So we have become God's work of art. We are reborn in the risen Lord, to live the kind of life we were called to, from the beginning. ▱

Salesian Reading Leader to choose from pages 62 - 68. ▱

Focus for Faith-Sharing

How many strands of hope can you see in the events of your day? ▱

Magnificat see page 59.

Intercessions

Lord, be with all young people at the end of this day.
R May they find inspiration to give their lives generously.

Lord, be with those who are unhappy in their work.
R May they find deeper meaning in their lives by listening to the Spirit.

Lord, be with parents separated from their children.
R May they maintain their love and continue to build bridges.

Our Father

Final Prayer

Lord, be with us in this evening hour. Help us to count our blessings rather than count the cost of this day in your service. Keep us in touch with the strands of your spirit woven through your people and plans. Even though we do not understand each twist and turn of life, help us trust you to weave something wonderful out of this ordinary day. We ask this through Christ Our Lord. **Amen**

Blessing

Spirit of God, woven through our life   *R Bring us peace*

Wisdom of God, hidden in each person   *R Keep us learning*

Son of God, raised through death to life   *R Renew our hope*

Week Three

Saturday

This is a slow contemplative praying of the Sunday scripture that leads towards union with God, and is an ideal way of preparing for tomorrow's Eucharist. Its simplicity helps to uncover some of the spiritual rhythms at work in our lives. The prayer rests on an ability to listen to scripture with the heart and *hear the still small voice of God.* (1 Kings 19:12)

Opening Prayer
Lord, open my ears to hear your word. May these moments of silence help me to recognise your presence calling me to life. Calm my heart and mind with your still small voice. **Amen**

How the word touches me
The Gospel passage for Sunday is read aloud twice with a brief pause between readings. Listeners notice some segment or word from the passage that attracts them. A brief silence follows. The group is invited to share, without explanation, the word or phrase that attracted them.

How the word speaks to me
The passage is read aloud again by a different person. Silence follows for reflection, *Where do these words touch my life today?* All are invited to share briefly on what connections the story makes with their lives.

How am I challenged?
The passage is read again by a third voice. Silence follows, reflecting on the phrase, *these words challenge me to......in the days that lie ahead.* A longer sharing follows.

Ending
The leader invites the group to pray in silence for those on either side of them.

Final Prayer
Thank you Lord, for your abiding presence in each person's life, and in these words of scripture. Stay with us this evening and help us to rest in your presence tonight. **Amen**

Other Scripture texts to use: St Luke's Gospel

Wake up little girl	8:49-56
Samaritan	10:29-37
Lost Sheep	15:4-7
Providence	12:22-32
A Widow's Son	7:11-17
Suffering	9:22-26

Week Four

Seek Me and live

Amos 5:4

In the busyness of your day keep an eye on God.
Be like sailors, who get to the harbour by
looking up to the stars as well as looking
at where they are on their journey.

St Francis de Sales

Week Four

Sunday

⌂ indicates a pause for reflection

Leader's Greeting
Stay with us Lord
It is Sunday evening
Time to rest in your risen presence. ⌂

Stay with us Lord
On the verge of a new week
Talk to us about your new life. ⌂

Thinking about the Day   see pages 60 - 61.

Offering
Lord of all life, I offer you the week that lies ahead. Help me to meet it with your timeless wisdom. Show me when to stick to routine and when to be flexible. Help me to stay focussed on your will rather than my own and bring me to the end of this week more deeply rooted in your life-giving love. ⌂

Choral Prayer
Philippians 3:7
Everything I thought was important
Has begun to change.

I need to let go of so many things
And leave more room for Christ Jesus.

Compared with knowing Christ face to face
Everything else is unimportant.

Living with less leaves more space
To embrace the risen Lord.

The struggle of the cross
Is the road to the risen Jesus.

I will hold a crucified hand
On the road to Resurrection.

Glory be to the Father…

Week Four

Scripture Reading

Matthew 13:47

God's kingdom is like a net full of fish, pulled out of the sea and landed on the shore. The fishermen sort the good fish into baskets and throw the rest back into the sea. If you have understood this parable you are like a wise steward, that knows how to draw out of his store of wisdom things old and things new, at the right time.

Salesian Reading   Leader to choose from pages 62 - 68. ⌐

Focus for Faith-Sharing
How flexible am I at following the promptings of the Spirit in my life? ⌐

Magnificat   see page 59.

Intercessions
Lord, we pray for all who will begin this week with anxiety and stress.
R Give them a strong sense of your presence in all that happens.

Lord, we pray for families preparing to sleep tonight.
R May they be at peace, may the sun not set on their anger.

Lord, be with those for whom this week will be their last.
R May they come home to you in peace.

Our Father

Final Prayer
Lord of creation, as we begin a new week, help us to be your partners in creating a better world. Keep us flexible and faithful in following the Gospel. Bring us safely to the end of this week at peace with you, richer in wisdom and closer to those around us. We ask this through Christ Our Lord. **Amen**

Blessing
Bless us with peace in all that will happen this week.   **Amen**
Give us courage in all that is uncertain.   **Amen**
Cheer our hearts with the gift of more time to do good.   **Amen**

Week Four

Monday

⌷ indicates a pause for reflection

Leader's Greeting
The Lord is with us in each minute of every day
Each breath is taken in God's presence
We live and breathe his love right now. ⌷

Bring us back to the centre of our life this evening Lord
Return us to the source of all love and inspiration
May your Spirit breathe through us in this evening prayer. ⌷

Thinking about the Day   see pages 60 - 61.

Offering
Lord, who walked with Adam and Eve in the garden, in the cool of the evening, walk with me through my day. Help me not to hide from your presence in what I remember of today. May I recognise humbly what I need to learn and allow you to be my guide. ⌷

Choral Prayer
Psalm 30

You deserve all the thanks Lord
You pulled me out of the mess I had made.

I called to you from the depth of my need
And you put me back together again.

Sing God's praises you saints
Thank God for his saving wisdom.

When things were going along well
I felt no need of God at all.

So proud of myself until God turned away
Then I fell flat on my face.

When I thought my life was over
You turned my mourning into dancing.

Lord, I cannot keep quiet about your goodness to me
I can never thank you enough.

Glory be to the Father…

Week Four

Scripture Reading

1 Thessalonians 5:13

Try to get along with each other in the community. Warn those who are doing too little, encourage those who are anxious, and reach out to those who are burdened. Be patient with each person and sensitive to individual needs. When you get on each others' nerves, don't answer back without thinking. Look for the best in others, and try to bring it to the surface for the good of the whole community. Stay cheerful whatever happens, thanking God for everything. This is the way people are called to live the life of the risen Jesus.

Salesian Reading   Leader to choose from pages 62 - 68. 📖

Focus for Faith-Sharing

How have people hidden and revealed God's presence today? 📖

Magnificat   see page 59.

Intercessions

For those who live alone or on the edge of the community.
R May the experience of a friendly face connect them back to life.

For those weighed down by anxiety.
R May they learn to trust again through faith, and the encouragement of friends and family.

For those who work too hard.
R May they find more satisfaction in doing less, and sharing responsibility when they need help.

Our Father

Final Prayer

Father, thank you for the friends and communities that support your Spirit in people. Help us to contribute honestly and generously to the community, and the network of friends and family in which we live. Move our hearts to offer both support and challenge to others, as we share our journey towards the risen Lord. **Amen**

Blessing

May the Lord give you peace with friends and neighbours.   **Amen**
May you find God's face in the faces of friends and enemies.   **Amen**

Week Four

Tuesday

⌂ indicates a pause for reflection

Leader's Greeting
Bread of life, feed us with your word
Tree of life, support us with your wisdom
Silence of God, surround us this evening. ⌂

Be with us as we gather the pieces of the day
Bring your wisdom to our experience
And sift our lives with your love. ⌂

Thinking about the Day   see pages 60 - 61.

Offering
Lord, like a child with its Father, I bring you the broken pieces of the day, and the plans that worked out well. Take the fragments of this day, and build them into your plan for a better world. Take my life, and let it be completely at the disposal of your love and wisdom this evening. ⌂

Choral Prayer
Psalm 72

Lord, bring your justice into our world
And your wisdom to those who rule
Let this wisdom endure for generations
And fall like rain on parched ground.

Let peace and justice blossom like flowers
And stay fresh until the moon fails
Let God's wisdom soak the whole earth
From sea to sea through every land.

Cynicism and self interest will vanish
Vengeance will evaporate into thin air
All earth's rulers will give way
Before the light of God's wisdom.

God will rescue the poor from oppression
Protecting them from tyranny and torture
The harvest will be endless
With food for everyone on earth.

Glory be to the Father...

Week Four

Scripture Reading

Proverbs 3:13

You are blessed if you discover the importance of wisdom in your life, and develop a discerning heart. Wisdom of heart is worth more than any treasure or money in the bank. Nothing comes close to the treasure that wisdom offers. The road to contentment and long life opens up the paths of wisdom, and brings blessings to the whole community. For those who cling to wisdom she becomes the tree of life, for it is out of wisdom that God created the whole universe. 📖

Salesian Reading   Leader to choose from pages 62 - 68. 📖

Focus for Faith-Sharing

In what ways do I see God's wisdom at work around me? 📖

Magnificat   see page 59.

Intercessions

Lord, be with those who have made foolish mistakes today.
R May they leave their failings in your hands to be changed to good.

We pray for our rulers.
R May they promote a deeper wisdom and discernment in all their discussions and decisions.

We pray for parents and educators.
R May their wisdom of heart ease the anxieties of the young, and inspire them to trust God.

Our Father

Final Prayer

Lord of wisdom, be with us in this evening hour. Set us free from anxiety and fear as we approach the end of this day. Help us to see our lives today against an eternal horizon, and learn wisdom of heart. We ask this through Jesus our risen Lord. **Amen**

Blessing

May the Lord bless us with peace of mind.   **Amen**
And may we rest in a wise and loving Lord tonight.   **Amen**

Week Four

indicates a pause for reflection

Leader's Greeting
Lord, we come home to you this evening
To sit awhile with you
And talk about the day. 📖

We bring you our heart and our hands
Our feelings and our actions
And we leave them in your care. 📖

Thinking about the Day   see pages 60 - 61.

Offering
Lord, thank you for each event and conversation that has carried me deeper into life. Collect the confusion this day has created, and clarify the emotions and meanings I need to understand. Iron out the mistakes I have made. In your kindness, prepare me for another day of life with you, my Lord and God. 📖

Choral Prayer
Psalm 85

Bring us home to you Lord
Don't hold a grudge against us.

Help us make a new start
And put the past behind us.

Lord, show us your face
And our friendship can begin again.

If only we admit our failings
God's love can flow back in.

Love and truth will eventually embrace
Justice and peace will kiss in friendship.

Faithfulness flows through the universe
And justice falls from the heavens.

Goodness will come to life everywhere
And peace will blossom in God's footprints.

Glory be to the Father...

Week Four

Scripture Reading

1 Peter 4:7
Care for one another with honest love and with sincere hearts. Loving like this makes up for everything else that can go wrong. Be quick in kindness, and generous in hospitality, keeping cheerful as you do the right thing. Be generous with the special gifts you have to share and, like a good steward, use them for the benefit of everyone. If you are good with words, let them be God's words too. If you are a helper then help with God's own love in your heart. In that way God's goodness will shine through all that you do in Christ Jesus. 📖

Salesian Reading   Leader to choose from pages 62 - 68. 📖

Focus for Faith-Sharing
In what ways do you see God shining through others? 📖

Magnificat   see page 59.

Intercessions
We pray for those who are alone and feeling isolated tonight.
R May they find in God's presence the promise of home.

We pray for all who are displaced by war and poverty.
R May they see your love made visible in the hospitality of their hosts.

Lord, we pray for grandparents.
R May their generosity, despite failing energy, bring blessings on many generations of their family.

Our Father

Final Prayer
Lord, be with us as we end another day. Help us build fairness and generosity into our lives, so that your kingdom of love and justice might become more visible. Keep us humble and reverent with the mystery of your life, wherever we discover it during the day. We ask this in the name of Jesus our risen Lord. **Amen**

Blessing
May the road unfold in mystery before you.	**Amen**
May the Lord walk close by your side.	**Amen**
May your heart be on fire with God's love.	**Amen**

Week Four

Thursday

*indicates a pause for reflection

Leader's Greeting
As the day ebbs away Lord
Walk with us along this evening shore
Help us gather what the day has washed up.

Help us sift what the day gave us
Gather what is of lasting value
And ponder on its meaning for tomorrow.

Thinking about the Day   see pages 60 - 61.

Offering
Lord, the tide of your love flows secretly through each day. All that this day has offered, I give to you. Let it flow back into the sea of your love. Leave me tonight with the deep peace that comes from knowing you.

Choral Prayer
Colossians 1:15

In Jesus we see the face of God
The God who cannot be seen
In Jesus we see God's plan unveiled
A plan for the entire universe forever.

Every force of nature, every human power
Makes sense only in the light of Christ Jesus
Before time began Jesus existed
All creation holds together in Him.

Jesus is the beginning of the church
And He leads it each day in love
He is the first on the journey to Resurrection
In his wholeness we find our home.

Everything broken, unfinished and frustrated
Finds completion and meaning in Him
By the Cross and Resurrection of Jesus
Everything is brought into place in God's plan.

Glory be to the Father...

Week Four

Scripture Reading

Hebrews 12:1

We should let go of anything that holds us back, on the journey toward Jesus. We need to persevere, despite our weakness and bad habits, in the commitment we have made to God. Try not to lose sight of Jesus. On his road, he endured many trials and setbacks. He did not give up because of shame or opposition, and neither should you. Think of Christ's journey and draw strength from the risen Lord as you travel your road.

Salesian Reading

Leader to choose from pages 62 - 68.

Focus for Faith-Sharing

How do you feel God's plan has worked with you today?

Magnificat

see page 59.

Intercessions

We pray for those burdened with worry.
R May they be drawn to trust God with their future.

We pray for those consumed by anger tonight.
R May they find a new perspective in the cross of Christ.

We pray for those who have lost direction.
R May they find a guide and friend to walk with them.

Our Father

Final Prayer

Lord, stay with us this evening. As we draw this day to a close, and plan for tomorrow, sit with us awhile. Give us an eternal perspective on our choices today and tomorrow. Help us live in your goodness and enjoy the freedom of your children. We ask this through Christ Our Lord.

Amen

Blessing

Let the sea of God's presence touch our minds with peace. **Amen**
Let the evening shore silence the troubles in our hearts. **Amen**
May we be drawn back into the sea of God's goodness. **Amen**

Week Four

Friday

⌂ indicates a pause for reflection

Leader's Greeting
May God shield us with peace at the end of this day
May God support us with truth as we examine the day
May God teach us love through the events of the day. ⌂

Each person and problem has carried God's presence
Each space and interruption has brought God's goodness
We are surrounded by God's gifts every day. ⌂

Thinking about the Day   see pages 60 - 61.

Offering
Lord, I offer you all the plans I made at the start of this day. I offer you all
that happened. Make your plans succeed where mine have failed. May
we work better together tomorrow. ⌂

Choral Prayer
Ephesians 1:3

We praise God, our loving Father
For the gift of our brother Jesus Christ
Before time began, God had each of us in mind
As part of an eternal plan of loving kindness.

As God's sons and daughters
We are brought close by the love of Jesus
The dying and the rising of Jesus
Has set each of us free to be children of God.

We have been drawn into God's presence
Through the plan revealed in Jesus
A plan to bring everything into harmony
Through the Death and Resurrection of Jesus.

In the cross and Resurrection
We discover who we really are
We are claimed as God's own people
And given a place with Christ in heaven.

Glory be to the Father...

Week Four

Scripture Reading

Jeremiah 29:11

I will take care of you and bring you home says the Lord. I know what plans I have for you, plans for peace and not for disaster. I will never abandon you. When you call I will answer. When you pray I will listen. When you look for me, with all your heart, you will find me close by. 📖

Salesian Reading

Leader to choose from pages 62 - 68. 📖

Focus for Faith-Sharing

Count the blessings God has given you today. 📖

Magnificat

see page 59.

Intercessions

Lord, stay with the young and poor this evening.
R Open their hearts to hope and help us to meet their deepest needs.

Lord, stay with the elderly and weary this evening.
R Reassure them that your plans are still at work in their lives.

Lord, stay with those who are near death, and those who care for them.
R May they experience the presence of Jesus, as their guide.

Our Father

Final Prayer

Lord, walk with us into this evening and talk to our hearts about the day. Help us to recognise your footsteps in the highs and lows of life. Stay close to those we live and work with, so that your kingdom might come to life in all our relationships. We ask this through Christ Our Lord. **Amen**

Blessing

May God the Father bless us.   **Amen**
The Holy Spirit enlighten us all the days of our life. **Amen**
May the Lord Jesus protect us, body and soul.   **Amen**

Week Four

Saturday

This is a slow contemplative praying of the Sunday scripture that leads towards union with God, and is an ideal way of preparing for tomorrow's Eucharist. Its simplicity helps to uncover some of the spiritual rhythms at work in our lives. The prayer rests on an ability to listen to scripture with the heart and *hear the still small voice of God.* (1 Kings 19:12)

Opening Prayer
Lord, open my ears to hear your word. May these moments of silence help me to recognise your presence calling me to life. Calm my heart and mind with your still small voice. **Amen**

How the word touches me
The Gospel passage for Sunday is read aloud twice with a brief pause between readings. Listeners notice some segment or word from the passage that attracts them. A brief silence follows. The group is invited to share, without explanation, the word or phrase that attracted them.

How the word speaks to me
The passage is read aloud again by a different person. Silence follows for reflection, *Where do these words touch my life today?* All are invited to share briefly on what connections the story makes with their lives.

How am I challenged?
The passage is read again by a third voice. Silence follows, reflecting on the phrase, *these words challenge me to......in the days that lie ahead.* A longer sharing follows.

Ending
The leader invites the group to pray in silence for those on either side of them.

Final Prayer
Thank you Lord, for your abiding presence in each person's life, and in these words of scripture. Stay with us this evening and help us to rest in your presence tonight. **Amen**

Other Scripture texts to use: St John's Gospel
A good shepherd	10:11-16A
Boy with bread	6:5-15
Love Each Other	15:9-17
Washing the feet	13:1-5
Be One	17:20-23

Magnificat

My soul glorifies the Lord

And my spirit rejoices in God's saving presence.

For he has recognised my weakness,

And yet all people will call me blessed.

For God has done great things for me, holy is his name.

His compassion is all around for those who want to see it.

He has shown a new kind of strength

and scattered the proud-hearted.

He has exalted the simple and the ordinary.

He has seen and fed deep hungers

And ignored the rich and greedy.

He has not given up on his plan of salvation

As he promised to Abraham and his family in faith.

Glory be to the Father…

Thinking about the Day

With Mary
Mary stood solidly in God's love at the foot of the cross.
Have I felt a sense of God's presence in the challenges of the day?
Mary pondered in her heart things that didn't make sense to her.
Have I tried to live reflectively through the activity of the day?
Mary inspired Don Bosco to draw people together in a community.
Have I sensed God's presence as a bridge between people today?

Don Bosco's Spirituality
Don Bosco created a spirituality from four elements:
A Home:
Have I felt that I belonged today with those I am connected to?
How have I welcomed others and made them feel at home?
A Church:
Have I been aware of God, present in my own heart through this day?
Have I stopped briefly today, to focus on God, on what is happening?
A School:
Are there any lessons this day has taught me?
Am I committed to being open-minded, and to admitting mistakes?
A Playground:
How far have I relaxed with people today, and been spontaneous?
How much has humour and fun been part of my day?

With Don Bosco, the good shepherd of the young
Don Bosco invites us to an optimistic approach to all that happens.
Have I been positive and encouraging today?
Salesian spirituality is active and involved in life.
Have I stood on the side-lines of this day, rather than taking part?
Recognising God in the ordinary is a Salesian gift.
How have I used this gift today?
Jesus, the Good Shepherd is a key figure on our way to God.
Have I shepherded others towards what is life-giving today?
Young people in need were at the heart of Don Bosco's mission.
Has my heart turned to the needs of the young and the poor today?

With Reverence
Have I met this day with reverence for the mystery it holds?
Have I taken time with routines,
or have I rushed impatiently ahead and missed the peace they offer?
Have I appreciated the small repeated gestures, *hellos* and *goodbyes*,
and focussed on the people who have touched my day?
Have I squeezed too much into too few hours?

Thinking about the Day

With Loving Kindness
Where has love been offered today? Where has love been rejected?
Where has my heart been moved with kindness and compassion?
Was I able to respond, when my heart was moved in this way?
Have I allowed myself to receive kindness, affection, and praise?
What stops me from receiving loving kindness from others?

With Gentleness
Have I found myself cutting corners and doing things too quickly?
Have I cut people off mid-sentence, in the rush to move on?
Have I been hard on myself when things didn't work out?
Have I been hard on others when they have not met my standards?
Have I been gentle with creation, with tools, food and friends?
Have I been gentle with God's presence in me, and in others?

With an Anxious Heart
Have I been at peace during the day?
Has anxiety touched my day, and if so how did I deal with it?
Has my heart turned to God to ask for peace at any time today?
As I end the day, do I carry any frustration and disappointment?
Do I feel that God's providence has been with me today?
Is there anything I need to let go of, and give to God now?

With Body and Mind
In my body:
Have I been caught by tensions that have taken me away from God?
Has anger made a home in me, and drowned the quiet voice of God?
Has anxiety blocked my sense of God's presence in others?
In my mind and heart:
Have I planned so much that I have missed God in the interruptions?
Have I carried resentment that has blocked the hospitality of others?
Have I stopped to still my heart and mind, and connect with the Lord?

With the living Jesus
When I met selfishness, have I endured patiently?
In my shortcomings and limitations, have I seen the bright side?
When others are short-tempered, have I shown good humour?
When others fail to show appreciation, have I kept cheerful?
When someone turns me down, have I kept calm?
When someone helped me, have I been appreciative?
In answering others, have I spoken with kindness and honesty?

Salesian Readings

Mary, strong in love

We must live unfailingly in loyalty to Jesus, especially when we are overwhelmed with gloom, disgust or desolation. That is how it was with Mary the Mother of Jesus, on the day of the passion. Whilst surrounded by horror, crude insults and all the trauma of death, she stood solid in her love. Even when Jesus showed no sign of awareness, when his eyes closed, when the shadow of death fell across them all, Mary stood resolute in her love.

St Francis de Sales, Treatise 9:11

Mary, inspiring care for the young

Mary showed Don Bosco his field of work among the young, and was a constant inspiration and support. Don Bosco believed that Mary was somehow present in all his work, creating a sense of community and supporting each person on their journey to Jesus. It was under her inspiration that Don Bosco created the first community with young people in Turin, and developed the preventive system as a way to live and work together.

Salesian Constitutions 8 & 20

Held by God's Hand

If we reflect on it, God's presence has been holding us by the hand all the time. In fact we have never been cut off from God during the day. We have been settled in His presence all the time, and perhaps completely unconscious of God's closeness. We may have been like Jacob who said, "Look, I have been so close to God, held in his presence and providence and I did not know it".

Francis de Sales, Treatise 6:2

Optimism

A Salesian does not usually complain about the current times, but sees and says what is good in the world, especially when it concerns young people. Because our task is to witness to the good news, a Salesian tries to be cheerful and develop a balanced way of life, that celebrates and educates others, in a happiness that comes from holiness.

Salesian Constitution 17

Salesian Readings

Welcome the Word

For us the word of Jesus, listened to with faith, is a source of spiritual life. It is food for prayer, light to see God's will in the events of life, and strength to live our Salesian vocation faithfully. We try to welcome the word of Jesus as Mary did, and ponder it in our hearts, so that it will bear fruit in our lives and help us to live it with more energy.

Salesian Constitution 87

Emmaus

We sometimes think that when God breaks through into our lives he will appear surrounded by angels and heavenly music. In fact God often comes to us in the ordinary moments and is only recognised in retrospect. Jesus spent a lot of time in sharing meals, in being sociable. He was courageous in conversation, and seemed to enjoy ordinary events, and be able to see through to deeper needs and potential. The ordinariness of the meal at Emmaus, at the end of a long walk, was the very place where Jesus let His risen presence be recognised. It is as if Jesus is challenging us to find Him within our own relationships.

Via Lucis

The signs of the times

Salesian spirituality demands that we are realists and sensitive to the signs of the times in which we live. We are convinced that God speaks through the demands of time and place. In this spirit Salesian spirituality welcomes new initiatives and creativity. As Don Bosco said, "In those things which are for the benefit of young people in danger, or which serve to win souls for God, I push ahead to the point of recklessness."

Salesian Constitution 19

Gentleness

As soon as you realise that you are acting out of anger, counteract the feeling, with a conscious act of gentleness, toward the person who is the focus of your anger. Just as the best remedy for lying is to disown the lie as soon as it is recognised, in the same way it is a good remedy to correct anger instantly. A prayer, made against a present and disturbing anger, ought to be a gentle prayer. Fresh wounds, after all, are easier to heal.

Francis de Sales
Introduction 3:8

Salesian Readings

The Shadow of our Lives
Meeting our own shortcomings sometimes seems like death, but as Jesus reminds us, the truth sets us free. As we grow older, the awareness of our fragility can lead to a deeper relationship with the mystery of Resurrection. It is as if we meet the Risen Lord in the shadow of our lives. He is there to walk with us through failure and weakness, and help us rise again through wisdom and humility. The path to Resurrection takes us all through the shadow side of life many times. It is often in shame and set-back, that we learn to put our hand into the wounded hands of Jesus and trust the road of Resurrection.

Via Lucis

Anger
When gentleness and humility are good and authentic in a person, they are guaranteed against the outbursts of anger and passion, that insults often provoke. This life is only a progressive journey towards a better life to come. So don't become angry with one another along the way. Let's walk in gentleness with our family and companions, with peaceful and kindly hearts.

St Francis de Sales,
Introduction 3:8

Balanced Love
One who knows he is loved will love in return, and one who loves can obtain anything, from even the most unruly young person. This confidence sets up an electric current between youngsters and adults. Hearts are opened, needs are made known. This love allows adults to put up with the weariness, the annoyance, the ingratitude and the troubles, that young people can cause. Jesus Christ did not crush the bruised reed nor quench the smouldering candle. He is our model. If we have this true love we will not seek anything beyond the will of God and the good of souls.

St John Bosco's
Letter, 1844

Belonging
Belonging means giving responsibility and holding young people to account. It means building friendships that will last into life. Belonging, longing to be all that a young person can be; with a little help from their friends. For Don Bosco, the skill of the adult is to create the environment that guarantees this safety and belonging among the young people in their care.

Ordinary Ways

Salesian Readings

Union with God

Union with God can be maintained by many small movements of the soul toward God. Just as a child in its mother's arms will snuggle closer with small movements, so the prayerful heart seeks closer union with God. At other times union is achieved by a constant and almost unconscious movement of the soul toward God. A huge heavy lump of lead or stone, free from all restrictions will tend to sink, bit by bit into the ground. The prayerful heart, once it is joined to God, sinks deeper and deeper into union with Him.

St Francis de Sales Treatise 7:1

Walking with the Young

We are called to walk alongside young people even when they are walking in the wrong direction! We are to be present with them, accepting them wherever they are, listening to their story, feeling their hopes and their disappointments. We move at their pace, respecting their dignity and freedom. We seek together to become aware of the Risen One present in our lives.

M T Winstanley, Don Bosco's Gospel Way

Contemplatives in action

In working for the good of young people, we are drawn into an experience of the Fatherhood of God, and are reminded of God's presence in our work. As scripture says, *Apart from me, you can do nothing*. We are challenged to deeper union with God, and to maintain a heart to heart communion with a felt presence of the risen Christ. In listening for the Spirit and constantly trying to do the most loving thing, we become contemplatives in action.

Salesian Constitution 12

No rushing

Nothing done impulsively and in a hurry is ever done well. As the ancient proverb says, we *must work with peaceful hearts*. He who hurries, says Solomon, *runs the risk of stumbling and hurting themselves.* We always do things fast enough when we do them well. Drones make a lot of noise but they only make wax. Rivers that run deep and slow, carry huge boats, but shallow turbulent rivers bring ruin and destruction to the land. In all your plans, rely on the providence of God, through which alone your plans will succeed.

St Francis de Sales, Introduction 3:10

Salesian Readings

Gentle Authority
Try to be friendly and gentle in approaching everyone. Gentleness is a virtue well loved by Jesus. Whatever you do or say, show a well mannered kindness, not only to those in authority, but especially to those in the community that have offended you, or who look upon you with an unkindly eye. He who will not bear gently with another's defects will never achieve true love. There is no one on earth who has no faults, however good they may be. Therefore if you wish others to bear your defects, you should begin by bearing the defects of others.

St John Bosco's Letter, 1885

An unknown way
The true way of following God is to walk by a way that we do not know. When it seems that everything is upside down within us, that is the time to practise trust in God. We should keep living a life of love and not struggle to know the reason for our confusion. Instead we should walk each day in abandonment to God's goodness. When God takes away the consolation of His presence we should join Jesus on the cross and say, 'Thy will be done'.

Conference 26, Jane Frances de Chantal

Busyness
There is, I think, a danger of being too busy being Samaritans to listen to the word with silent attentiveness, to go to the mountain of prayer. Often our busyness is tinged with over-anxiety, inducing stress and tension. In some cases one can detect symptoms of a workaholic, incipient or verging on chronic. This can entail a blurring of perspectives, a loss of true focus. When there are clashes of priorities, it tends to be prayer which is jettisoned.

Don Bosco's Gospel Way

Learning
For Don Bosco everyone is potentially a teacher. In a school, it may be the dinner-ladies or the caretaker that help a young person to learn a vital lesson in life. In a parish, the old person sitting quietly at the back who talks and smiles to young people may be a profound teacher of wisdom. So often, in Don Bosco's mind, it was young people themselves who were the best teachers, speaking with an honesty and immediacy that few adult friends could match.

Ordinary Ways

Salesian Readings

Celebration

As adults we may take ourselves too seriously. When we do so, we are in danger of losing the energy we need to be ourselves. We may even feel threatened by young people's exuberance. Don Bosco encouraged his co-workers to be young with the young. He wanted young people to grow to maturity and yet still have access to that youthful inner energy that could let them play and simply be. He saw play as an act of faith. Each person can only carry a small part of the world.

Ordinary Ways

Meaning

We are not in control of the invasion of mystery into the lives of young people, but we must not miss it. We simply need to be aware, like the disciples after the Resurrection, that *It is The Lord!* standing on the shore of our awareness. Feeding all of us with the bread of his presence among young people. It is this network of friendship that forms the church that holds God's presence.

Ordinary Ways

Signs of Hope

In daily experience we will find people and situations where peace, new life and hope suddenly break through. They are moments when the light of the Resurrection shines through a good friendship or an honest word. They are probably more common than we think. As followers of a Risen Lord there is a challenge for us to be signs of hope. We can help liberate others from their fear by an honest friendship and silent prayer that invites the Risen Lord into every conversation.

Via Lucis

Revelation

There are many moments, scattered through our lives, when we come alive. We grow in awareness, and suddenly see something that was always there, in a totally new way. That sudden insight is rare for an individual, but even more amazing when it happens for a whole group. The men and women in the upper room spent their time waiting, reflecting and in silence. All of a sudden they received inspiration as a group. They were overcome with the joy and energy of insight and wisdom. They would never see the events of Jesus' life in the same way again.

Via Lucis

Salesian Readings

Being Child Like

Act like small children who, with one hand hold tight to their Father, and with the other lean in to pick berries from among the thorn hedges. In the same way, as you manage the ordinary things of each day, hold fast with one hand to your Father and, from time to time, turn to your Father to see if your actions are pleasing Him. Take care not to let go of that hand in order to gather more. If you let go, you may well fall flat on your face.

Francis de Sales, Introduction 3:10

New Ways

How many times has the Lord stood on the lake-shore of our lives and called out to us to do things differently? How many times have we heard the voice of a stranger go straight to our hearts? To recognise, like St John, that *It is the Lord!* The Risen Jesus seems to slip through our lives and offer us new life in interruptions, coincidences and setbacks. This new offer of Resurrection is always challenging us to look to a wider horizon. It is never a life that can be contained or tamed by plans and procedures. The risen life searches us out, even as we struggle towards it. It is a life that asks us to be open, and ready to move in new ways. We recognise the Lord, inviting us to meet him in ordinary moments, like breakfast.

Via Lucis

Hidden in Christ

Love is the active, driving force of the soul and spiritual life. Love gives life, energy, sensitivity and direction to our spiritual lives. So, as soon as we have given our soul to Christ in love, we have in that one act given the whole of our spiritual life into Christ's safe keeping. For now that spiritual life is hidden with Christ and lived by active faith. So where is the good of being caught up into God's love in prayer, when our activities are trapped in the love of earthly and shallow concerns?

Francis de Sales, Treatise 7:7

Sources of Readings

Trust the Road by David O'Malley SDB

Ordinary Ways by David O'Malley SDB

Via Lucis by David O'Malley SDB

Don Bosco's Gospel Way by Michael T Winstanley SDB

Obtainable from
Don Bosco Publications
Thornleigh House
Sharples Park
Bolton
BL1 6PQ
Tel 01204 308811 Fax 01204 306868
Email michael@salesians.org.uk

and from our website
www.don-bosco-publications.co.uk

or from Christian Bookshops